MAPPING EARTHFORMS

Volcanoes

Melanie Waldron

www.heinemann.co.uk/library
Visit our website to find out more information about Heinemann Library books.

To order:
☎ Phone 44 (0) 1865 888066
▯ Send a fax to 44 (0)1865 314091
▯ Visit the Heinemann Library Bookshop at www.heinemann.co.uk/library to browse our catalogue and order online.

First published in Great Britain by Heinemann Library, Halley Court, Jordan Hill, Oxford OX2 8EJ, part of Harcourt Education. Heinemann Library is a registered trademark of Harcourt Education Ltd.

Editorial: Joanna Talbot
Design: Richard Parker and Q2A Solutions
Illustrations: Jeff Edwards
Picture Research: Hannah Taylor
Production: Duncan Gilbert

Originated by Chroma Graphics (Overseas) Pte. Ltd
Printed and bound in China by Leo Paper Group

ISBN 978 0 431 10993 0
11 10 09 08 07
10 9 8 7 6 5 4 3 2 1

British Library Cataloguing in Publication Data
Waldron, Melanie
Volcanoes. – (Mapping Earthforms)
552.2'1
A full catalogue record for this book is available from the British Library.

Acknowledgements
The publishers would like to thank the following for permission to reproduce photographs: Alamy Images/Greg Vaughn p. **11** (bottom); Corbis pp. **20** (Hubert Stadler), **11** (top, Jose Fuste Raga), **5**, **24** (Reuters), **16** (Steve Terrill); Getty Images pp. **25** (AFP), **19** (Aurora), **7** (Stone), **18** (Taxi), **27** (The Image Bank); Photolibrary pp. **17** (James H Robinson), **13**, **14** (Pacific Stock), **4** (Tammy Peluso); Reuters/ Romeo Ranoco pp. **12**, **21**; Rex Features/ Sipa Press pp. **15**, **23**; Science Photo Library/Tom Van Sant, Geosphere Project, Planetary Visions p. **9**.

Cover photograph reproduced with permission of Science Photo Library/Bernhard Edmaier.

Every effort has been made to contact copyright holders of any material reproduced in this book. Any omissions will be rectified in subsequent printings if notice is given to the publishers.

Contents

Any words appearing in the text in bold, **like this**, are explained in the Glossary. You can find the answers to Map Active questions on page 29.

What is a volcano?

What can hurl lumps of melted rock hundreds of metres into the air? What can blow itself apart and destroy everything in its reach? The answer is – a volcano. Volcanoes are mountains or hills that have been created by layers of lava and ash. They can be very dangerous and unpredictable landforms.

Volcanoes can be found all over the world. Some volcanoes are more powerful than others, and some are more **active** than others. This means that they are more likely to erupt. There are many ancient volcanoes that are said to be **extinct**. This means that they are unlikely ever to erupt again. **Dormant** volcanoes may not have erupted for hundreds of years, but they show some signs that they may erupt again in the future.

◀ When volcanoes erupt they can rip themselves apart, like this eruption of Rabual in Papua New Guinea in 1994.

▲ Living in the shadow of an active volcano like Mount Mayon in the Philippines is a reality for many people. How would you feel about living this close to an active volcano?

How have volcanoes formed?

The ground under your feet is not as solid as you might think! There are cracks and openings in Earth's **crust**. At these places volcanoes can form. Below Earth's surface it is so hot that the rock has melted into runny material called **magma**. When this material pushes its way to the surface of Earth it is called **lava**. Volcanoes are formed when lava spills out and hardens to form rock.

Life beneath a volcano

You might think that people would not want to live anywhere near a volcano. In fact, all across the world people can be found living close to volcanoes – even active ones! They have **adapted** their lives to coping with the threat of an eruption. Many plants and animals are also found living on the ever-changing slopes of active volcanoes.

Volcanoes of the world

Volcanoes are found in many places across the world, where the **magma** below the **crust** manages to reach the surface. Earthquakes usually occur in the same places as volcanic eruptions. They both usually occur where parts of Earth's crust meet each other.

Below Earth's crust is a deep layer of **molten** rock called the **mantle**. This is where magma is found. Earth's crust sits on top of this layer of magma. The crust is not one solid lump of rock. In fact, it is made up of a number of different-sized sections of rock called **tectonic plates**. These plates move very slowly over the surface of Earth – up to 10 centimetres (4 inches) every year. Volcanoes and earthquakes usually occur at plate boundaries, where the plates meet.

▼ This map shows the location and names of the largest tectonic plates that cover Earth's crust. The location of **active** volcanoes and earthquakes are also shown.

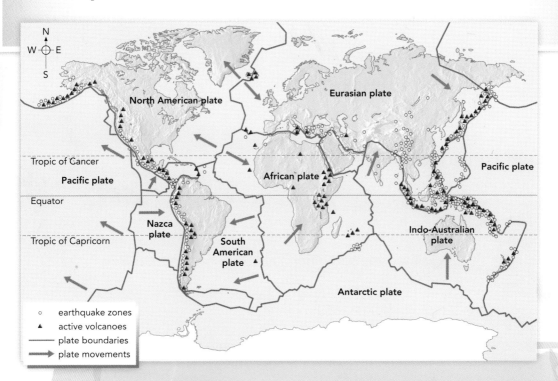

MAP ACTIVE

The map shows that most volcanoes and earthquakes occur at plate boundaries. Can you find two areas where this is not the case?

▶ It is hard to believe that the ground beneath our feet is not completely solid. However, this photo of the San Andreas Fault in California, USA, clearly shows that there is movement in Earth's crust.

Volcanoes usually occur where plates are either moving away from each other or moving towards each other. Earthquakes usually occur where plates are moving towards each other or where they slide past each other. All of these plate boundaries are called **active zones**.

Sometimes volcanoes can form in the middle of plates, away from plate boundaries. This happens when Earth's crust lies above an extremely hot area of magma called a **hot spot**. The magma is so hot that it rises up through the mantle and pushes through the crust. The islands of Hawaii, in the middle of the Pacific Ocean, are all volcanoes that have been formed in this way.

Active zone volcanoes

The giant **tectonic plates** that cover Earth's surface float like rafts on the hot **magma** inside Earth. The magma is so hot that **currents** start to flow in it. These currents cause the tectonic plates to move slowly over the surface. All of these movements are called **plate tectonics**.

Constructive boundaries

Where two plates are slowly moving away from each other, a gap is created between the plates. Magma from below the surface rises up to fill this gap. As the magma explodes or oozes out on to the surface as **lava**, it slowly cools. This creates new **crust** to fill the gap, and so these plate boundaries are called **constructive boundaries**. Volcanoes form when the lava builds up, layer after layer, to create mountains or ridges of mountains. The magma has to rise up the volcano before coming out as lava.

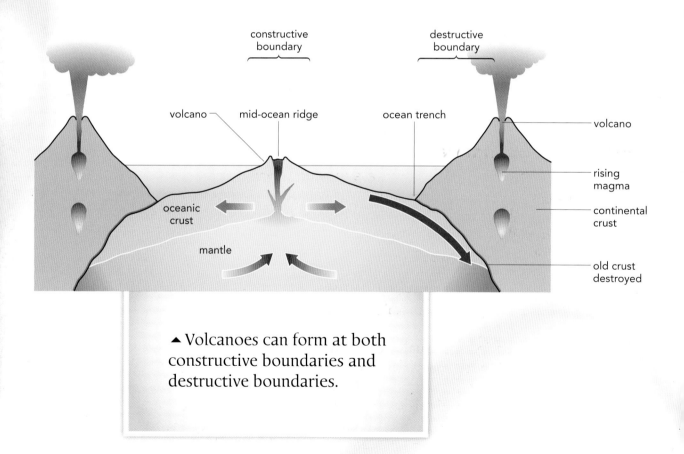

constructive boundary

destructive boundary

volcano — mid-ocean ridge

ocean trench

volcano

rising magma

oceanic crust

continental crust

mantle

old crust destroyed

▲ Volcanoes can form at both constructive boundaries and destructive boundaries.

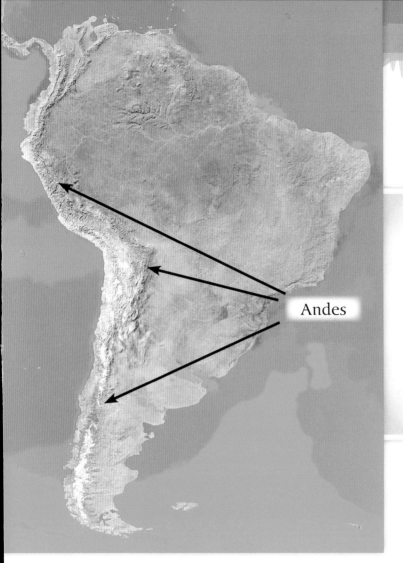

Andes

◀ The Andes are mountains that run the length of South America. They formed millions of years ago at the boundary between the Nazca Plate and the South American Plate.

Destructive boundaries

Volcanoes can also form where plates are moving towards each other. When two plates collide like this, one of the plates can be pushed below the other. As this crust is pushed down into the **mantle**, the hot temperatures start to melt the rock and the old crust is destroyed. These boundaries are called **destructive boundaries** for this reason. As the old crust gradually turns into magma, this extra magma builds up pressure in the mantle. The magma forces its way to the surface, eventually exploding out as lava. As more and more layers of lava cool on the surface, volcanoes form.

Constructive boundaries are usually found in the middle of oceans. Here the crust is thinner than on the **continents**. The plates can easily be pulled apart by the currents in the mantle. The Mid-Atlantic Ridge is a line of mostly underwater volcanoes that run up the middle of the Atlantic Ocean. Destructive boundaries are usually found on the edges of continents, where the thicker continental crust pushes the thinner oceanic crust below it. The Andes is a line of mountains and volcanoes along a destructive boundary.

Inside a volcano

Volcanoes form where **magma** from inside the **mantle** manages to rise to the surface. Often the magma sits just below the surface, in a huge **magma chamber**, until it is able to push up and out. Pressures inside these magma chambers can be huge, until eventually the magma rises up and the pressure is released.

Layers of lava

As the magma reaches the surface as **lava**, it pours out over the surrounding rock and begins to cool and harden. Sometimes ash is also thrown out. As layer after layer of lava cools and hardens, a volcano begins to form. The volcano is made up of lots of layers of lava and ash, laid down each time the volcano erupts. Magma rises up through the middle of the volcano, called the **vent**. Sometimes little cracks form in the old lava layers and magma can push through these to make side vents. Small eruptions can occur on the volcano slopes where these side vents reach the surface. These form small cones called **parasitic cones**.

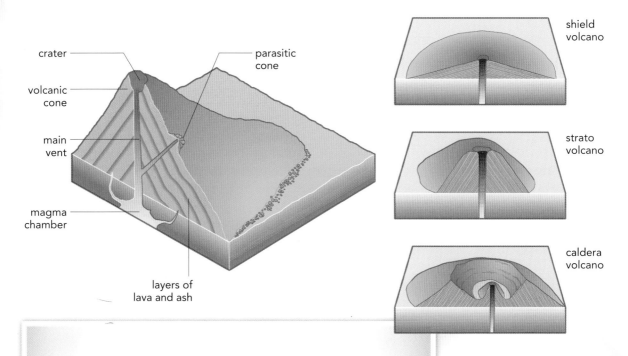

crater

parasitic cone

volcanic cone

main vent

magma chamber

layers of lava and ash

shield volcano

strato volcano

caldera volcano

▲ Different types of volcano will erupt in different ways and create different landforms.

◀ Strato volcanoes, such as Mount Fuji in Japan, have very steep sides.

Volcano types

There are three common types of volcanoes, depending on the type of lava and the force of the volcanic eruption.

- Shield volcano. These volcanoes form where the lava is quite runny. This means that the eruptions are relatively gentle because the lava simply oozes from the magma chamber and the vent whenever the pressure rises. As it is runny, the lava can travel long distances before it cools and hardens. This results in a very wide volcano with gently sloping sides.

- Strato volcano. Where the lava is stickier, eruptions can be more violent. This is because the lava can contain lots of gas bubbles. The build-up of gas can create higher pressures inside the volcano, so the lava can explode out. As it is sticky, the lava does not flow far before cooling. This means that the volcano will have steeply sloping sides.

- **Caldera** volcano. When an eruption is so powerful it blows the top of the volcano right off, a huge crater called a caldera can form. Eventually, a smaller volcanic cone can start to build up in the middle of this large crater.

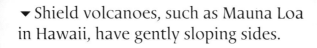

▼ Shield volcanoes, such as Mauna Loa in Hawaii, have gently sloping sides.

Volcano erupts!

Scientists are still not completely sure about the exact causes of a volcanic eruption. However, there are some ideas about the steps in an eruption and the **triggers** for an eruption.

The build-up of pressure in the **magma chamber** below the volcano is often the main trigger for an eruption. This can be caused by movements in Earth's **tectonic plates**, by earthquakes near the magma chamber, or by old **crust** melting and increasing the amount of **magma**. As the pressure increases, the magma escapes up through the **vent** of the volcano.

▼ Mount Mayon in the Philippines showing warning signs of eruption in August 2006.

◀ When a volcano erupts, the pressure inside the magma chamber is released and the magma explodes out as lava.

Blowing the top

In the top parts of a volcanic vent, there is usually a plug of old, cooled **lava** that was left behind after the last eruption. This plug is a bit like a cork in a bottle of wine. As the magma rises up the vent, the plug holds it back. Sometimes the magma is held there until the pressure drops and the magma sinks back. At other times, however, the pressure of the magma pushes through the plug and an eruption takes place.

Erupt or not?

Whether or not an eruption takes place is often due to the amount of gas in the magma. Thick magma can have lots of gas trapped inside, which can create very high pressures. This means the volcano is more likely to erupt. Some people have suggested that the weather can cause eruptions. They argue that if there is air at low pressure above a volcano, there will be less force pushing down on the surface and so the magma will be more easily able to push through the surface. It has been suggested that the eruption of Mount Pinatubo in 1991 may have been triggered by typhoon Yunya. The centre of the typhoon, where air pressures are very low, passed over the volcano just as it erupted. However, it is very difficult to prove this.

Eruption!

When a volcano erupts, lava and hot rocks are thrown from the vent. Huge clouds of ash and gas can rise from the vent, hundreds of metres into the sky. An eruption can last for just a few days, or it can continue rumbling for years!

Effects of eruption

Every volcano is different, and every volcanic eruption is also different. The effects of an eruption vary enormously depending on the type of volcano, the violence of the eruption, and the distances between communities of people and the volcano.

Lava flows

Most volcanic eruptions result in **lava** flows. These can be small and slow-moving or large and fast-moving. Lava will burn everything in its path including houses, trees, and cars. Gradually the lava will start to cool and will eventually harden to form a new ground surface.

Volcanic bombs

Some volcanoes throw out chunks of rock, from small pebbles to huge boulders more than a metre wide. These rock "bombs" can be very hot and even partly **molten**, and they can create fires wherever they land. They can be thrown huge distances – up to a few kilometres. Because of this they can often cause more damage than lava flows, which may not move far from the volcano.

Pyroclastic flows

Pyroclastic flows are often the biggest killers in volcanic eruptions. They are huge clouds of ash, mixed with hot, poisonous gases and volcanic bombs, that blast down the volcano's sides. They can travel at more than 160 kilometres (100 miles) per hour, ripping trees out of the soil and flattening buildings. They are deadly. Anyone caught in a pyroclastic flow is highly unlikely to survive.

▶ Lava flows are almost impossible to divert or control. How would you feel if you saw a flow of lava heading towards your house?

◀ Lahars can be extremely dangerous. A volcanic eruption in Columbia in 1985 set off lahars that killed over 23,000 people.

Lahars

When pyroclastic flows mix with water, **lahars** can form. The water may come from heavy rainfall during the eruption, from inside the volcano, or from ice and snow on the volcano sides that melt in an eruption. Lahars are volcanic mudflows, and they too can be deadly. They can crush and cover buildings, trees, and cars, and the mud can set as hard as concrete when it stops flowing.

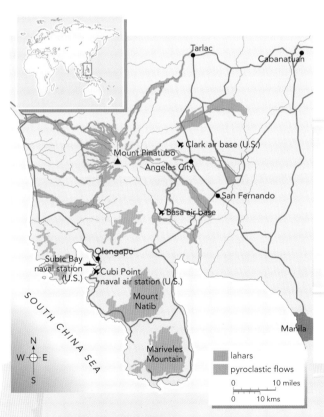

◀ This map shows the areas affected by lahars and pyroclastic flows in the 1991 Mount Pinatubo eruption in the Philippines.

MAP ACTIVE

How might this map help planners and builders in future development projects around the volcano?

Eruption! Mount St Helens

Mount St Helens is an **active** strato volcano in the Cascade Mountains, Washington, USA. Before 1980, there had been a few small eruptions in the last 100 years, and the last one happened in 1921. Then, on 18 May 1980, the volcano was ripped apart by one of the most powerful eruptions of the 20th century.

The build-up

Volcanologists had been monitoring activity on Mount St Helens for many years before the 1980 eruption. The volcano appeared to be inactive. Then, in March 1980, small earthquakes below the volcano were detected. These increased in strength through April and into May, and several small eruptions of steam and gases were reported. The governor of Washington declared a state of emergency and the world held its breath, waiting for a big eruption.

▼ The eruption of Mount St Helens in 1980 was one of the most powerful eruptions of the 20th century.

▲ Thousands of trees were blasted flat by the force of the Mount St Helens eruption.

However, by 17 May all earthquakes and eruptions had stopped, and the authorities allowed some people back into the area around the volcano. Suddenly, without warning, at 8.32 a.m. on 18 May, an earthquake caused part of the volcano to collapse. The rock debris slid down the mountainside – filling a river valley. As the pressure on the volcano was released by this collapsing rock, the volcano was able to explode outwards. A **pyroclastic flow** – an extremely hot blast of **molten** rock, harder rock, gas, and steam – raced down the mountain, blasting trees flat. A huge column of ash rose high into the sky, visible from many kilometres away. Melted snow and ice mixed with the ash and rock to create **lahars** that sped down the slopes.

The after-effects

The rock debris, pyroclastic flow, and lahars did terrible damage. Fifty-seven people were killed and 250 homes were destroyed. Roads, railways, and bridges were also wiped out. Thousands of animals were killed and the beautiful landscape around the volcano was devastated. The blast destroyed the top of the mountain and lowered its height from 2,950 metres (9,700 feet) to 2,550 metres (8,400 feet).

Since the 1980 eruption, Mount St Helens has erupted a few more times. However, these have been very small in comparison and have been mostly confined to the volcano's crater.

Volcanoes and wildlife

On the slopes of volcanoes that have not erupted for hundreds or thousands of years, plants and animals live and grow just like on any other mountain in the area. In fact, most plants can grow extremely well on volcanic soil! This is because volcanic soils are very **fertile**, due to the rich **minerals** in volcanic rocks and ash. Over time the rock and ash is broken down to form soil, and plants grow well in these mineral-rich areas.

Barren land

Of course, it is a very different story after a volcanic eruption. If there have been **lava** flows down the side of a mountain, the plants are burned and the ground is covered over by **molten** rock. Any animals living in these areas that cannot escape in time are killed. Eventually the molten rock cools and hardens, forming a **barren** landscape of bare rock. After a **pyroclastic flow**, trees and other vegetation can be blasted flat, and layers of ash and rock can settle on the ground.

▲ The high ash content of volcanic soils makes them very fertile and ideal for growing crops such as this tea, growing in the shadow of Mount Fuji, Japan.

New life begins

Plants soon begin to appear on the hardened lava. They take root in the small cracks on the rock surface, where water can collect and the roots can grip on to little particles of rock. Plants such as these are called "**pioneer species**". Over time, and depending on the **climate**, patches of soil begin to form and other plants can grow. In a warm, wet climate (for example in Indonesia) this can happen quickly – within tens of years. In a cold, dry climate (for example in Alaska) it may take hundreds of years.

Many people have realized the benefits of fertile volcanic soils. In Hawaii, for example, crops of sugar cane, pineapple, coffee, and macadamia nuts have been planted on these rich soils. Animals, too, can benefit. The rich vegetation on the fertile slopes provides good homes and food supplies for many animals.

Living in the shadow

Volcanic eruptions can be deadly and can cause huge amounts of damage. Why, then, do people continue to live close to volcanoes that are known to be **active**?

In some countries, such as Japan, mountains and volcanoes dominate the land. Only a narrow strip of flat coastal land surrounds them. Towns and cities have grown up along these narrow strips of land because the high ground is too steep to build on. This means that the towns and cities will always be near to the volcanoes. Many communities practise safety drills just in case one of the volcanoes erupts.

The pull of the volcano

In many countries there are very **fertile** soils found on the slopes of volcanoes. Because these soils are so productive, people choose to live close to the volcano so they can farm the land.

▼ This town in Chile lies in the shadow of Villarrica. The local people have lived with the threat of eruption for many years, since the last eruption that occurred in 1999.

▲ Practising evacuation and rescue plans in towns near a volcano can make all the difference when it comes to a real eruption. Here in Legazpi in the Philippines, school pupils practise moving to safety.

Some volcanoes behave very predictably, and people become used to the types of eruption that occur. This makes people feel safe because they can settle in areas where they are sure the eruptions will not reach. This is the case for Mount Etna on the island of Sicily in the Mediterranean. It is an active volcano, but most of the time it just smokes and erupts gently. The volcano has even been given the nickname "the friendly giant". This is because in the last 3,500 years, only 73 people have been killed in its eruptions.

Case study – Mount Merapi, Java, Indonesia

Close to one million people live within 32 kilometres (20 miles) of Mount Merapi, one of the most active volcanoes in the world. Many people make a living by growing crops on the fertile soils surrounding the volcano. The volcano erupts frequently, however, with very large eruptions happening every 50 or 60 years. The local people are reluctant to move and instead choose to risk living with the volcano. Many people regard Mount Merapi as a spiritual volcano, and they offer prayers and carry out rituals to the volcano, asking it to protect them.

A way of life – Montserrat

Montserrat is a small island in the Caribbean Sea, lying between Antigua and Guadeloupe. It is about 18 kilometres (11 miles) long and 11 kilometres (7 miles) wide. The island is very mountainous, lush, and green. Before 1995, many of its inhabitants made a living farming vegetables, livestock, and cotton, and others worked in industries such as food processing and electrics. There were also a number of office workers and people employed in the large tourism industry. In 1995, after 350 years of silence from its volcanoes, everything changed for the people of Montserrat.

In July 1995, a volcano in the Soufriere Hills suddenly erupted and thousands of people were forced to leave their homes and move to safer areas. As the island is so small, many people fled to neighbouring islands and to the United States and the United Kingdom. However, the worst was yet to come.

▶ Almost two-thirds of Montserrat were declared unsafe and made into an exclusion zone in 1997. The entire population now lives in the northern safe zone, or abroad in other countries.

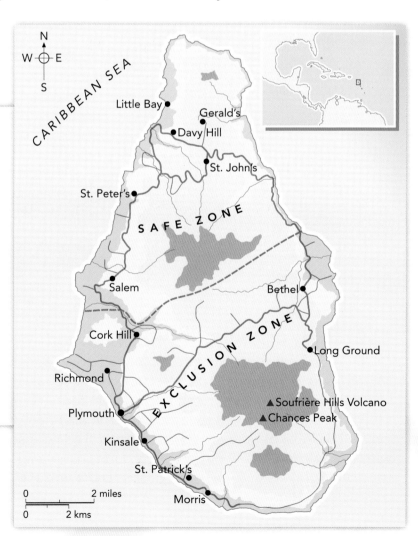

CARIBBEAN SEA

Little Bay
Gerald's
Davy Hill
St. John's
St. Peter's
SAFE ZONE
Salem
Bethel
Cork Hill
EXCLUSION ZONE
Long Ground
Richmond
▲ Soufrière Hills Volcano
Plymouth
▲ Chances Peak
Kinsale
St. Patrick's
0   2 miles
0   2 kms
Morris

▲ Montserrat's capital town, Plymouth, after the 1997 eruptions. Ash covers most of the town and many buildings have been destroyed.

In June 1997, the volcano erupted violently. The effects of this eruption devastated the island. Huge, hot **pyroclastic flows** swept down the volcano's sides and covered vast areas of the island. The capital town of Plymouth, to the west of the volcano, was abandoned as ash, hot rocks, and gases settled all over the town. In total 19 people were killed. The volcano continued to erupt for the next few years, leaving almost two-thirds of the island uninhabitable. This area was declared an "exclusion zone" and entry to the area was severely restricted.

Since 1997, many of the islanders have stayed away. The official population in 1991 was 10,639, and this had dropped to 4,482 in 2001. Many of the industries and business on the island have failed, and the economy of the island is now largely supported by aid from foreign countries. However, the residents that stayed have hope that the volcano will quieten down soon and that they will be able to rebuild their lives. The volcano has been fairly quiet since July 2003. Hopes are high that parts of the exclusion zone will be opened up. A new airport is already being built and there are plans to make the town of Little Bay the new capital.

Predicting volcanic eruptions

People will always live close to volcanoes, either because there is very little other land available or because they do not want to leave their homes and communities. However, modern technology can help to predict an eruption, so people can be warned to move to safety before an eruption happens.

Volcanologists use a variety of different methods to try to predict when a volcano will next erupt.

- Landscape changes. Scientists can use satellite images and photographs to examine any changes in the landscape around a volcano. Before many eruptions, the ground is seen to swell up slightly, due to the **magma** rising up towards the surface.

▼ Scientists must wear special suits to protect them from the heat and gases as they monitor volcanoes. It is an exciting, but very dangerous, job.

▲ Farmers work in their rice fields in Sleman, Indonesia, in June 2006. Above them, Mount Merapi shows warning signs of erupting.

- Patterning. By studying when eruptions happened in the past, scientists can work out if there are any patterns in the volcano's explosions. This can help predict when the next eruption might be due.
- Gas monitoring. Sensitive instruments can detect slight changes in the gases produced by a volcano. Levels of sulphur dioxide and carbon dioxide can rise before an eruption, so these instruments can alert people to this.
- Seismic monitoring. Many volcanic eruptions occur after slight earthquakes and earth tremors. Scientists can monitor quakes and tremors using instruments called seismometers, which pick up any movement.

Every volcano is different, however, and volcanoes are generally very unpredictable! Using a combination of the above methods is the best way to predict an eruption, but scientists cannot say for sure if or when a volcano will erupt.

Perhaps a more useful approach is to plan for when an eruption may happen. Evacuation and emergency plans can be created in towns and cities, so that everyone knows what to do in an eruption. Some communities may practise drills to make sure the plans work smoothly in real life.

Looking to the future

Volcanoes are places of great drama and beauty, but they can also be deadly. Volcanoes around the world will continue to erupt in the future, changing landscapes and affecting the lives of people living nearby. But could the world cope with a **supervolcano** eruption?

Scientists have identified around seven supervolcanoes around the world. A supervolcano is a huge volcano, often lying below the ground so that only the top parts show. In a supervolcano eruption, so much **lava**, gas, and ash are produced that the landscape is changed beyond recognition, and the **climate** of the whole world is affected. This is because the gases and ash in the atmosphere block out the Sun's rays and cause temperatures to drop.

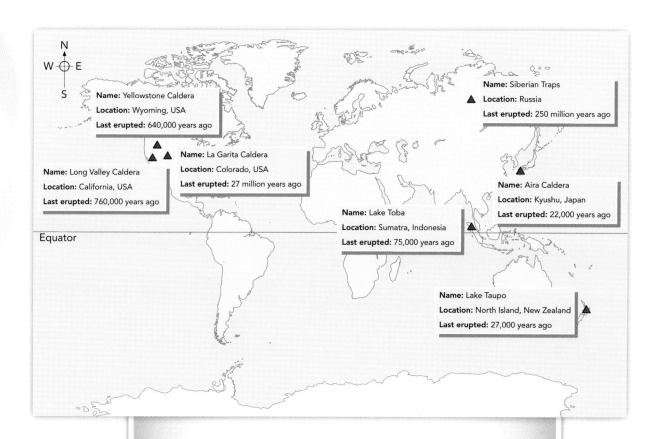

N
W ⊕ E
S

Name: Yellowstone Caldera
Location: Wyoming, USA
Last erupted: 640,000 years ago

Name: Siberian Traps
Location: Russia
Last erupted: 250 million years ago

Name: La Garita Caldera
Location: Colorado, USA
Last erupted: 27 million years ago

Name: Long Valley Caldera
Location: California, USA
Last erupted: 760,000 years ago

Name: Aira Caldera
Location: Kyushu, Japan
Last erupted: 22,000 years ago

Name: Lake Toba
Location: Sumatra, Indonesia
Last erupted: 75,000 years ago

Equator

Name: Lake Taupo
Location: North Island, New Zealand
Last erupted: 27,000 years ago

▲ Scientists think there are seven supervolcanoes around the world. Some are due to erupt sooner than others. Imagine if they all erupted at once!

▲ Underneath the natural beauty of Yellowstone National Park in Wyoming, USA, is there a huge volcano just waiting to erupt?

Supervolcanoes are different from other volcanoes. They do not have sloping sides rising high above Earth's **crust**. What makes a supervolcano is the size of the enormous **magma chamber** lying below it. Scientists estimate these magma chambers can be more than 10 kilometres (6 miles) in diameter. Because the magma chamber is so huge, the pressure that builds up inside them can be incredibly high – causing catastrophic eruptions.

The last Lake Toba supervolcano eruption in Indonesia took place around 75,000 years ago. The eruption plunged the entire world into darkness and cold, and scientists think around 60 per cent of the human population at the time was killed. The Yellowstone **Caldera** supervolcano in Wyoming had a massive eruption 2.1 million years ago. This spread ash over much of North America and changed weather systems across the world. It last erupted around 640,000 years ago, and some scientists say that it is due to erupt again. But don't worry, it shows no signs of erupting at the moment!

Volcano facts

The 10 worst volcanic eruptions, according to the number of people killed:

Rank	Volcano	Year	Deaths
1.	Tambora, Indonesia	1815	92,000
2.	Krakatau, Indonesia	1883	36,417
3.	Mount Pelee, Martinique	1902	29,025
4.	Ruiz, Colombia	1985	25,000
5.	Unzen, Japan	1792	14,300
6.	Laki, Iceland	1783	9,350
7.	Kelut, Indonesia	1919	5,110
8.	Galunggung, Indonesia	1882	4,011
9.	Vesuvius, Italy	1631	3,500
10.	Vesuvius, Italy	79	3,360

Based on data in *Volcanic Hazards: A Sourcebook on the Effects of Eruptions* by Russell J. Blong (Academic Press, 1984)

- Mount Kilauea in Hawaii is thought to be the world's most **active** volcano at the moment. It has been erupting almost non-stop since 1983.

- The word "volcano" comes from ancient Rome. Their name for the god of fire was Vulcan.

- On 23 May 1980, five days after Mount St Helens erupted, a film crew was dropped by helicopter on the mountain. Their aim was to film the destruction caused by the eruption. However, their compasses stopped working and they got lost. The volcano erupted two days later, but the film crew survived. They were eventually rescued on 27 May by National Guard helicopters. Their film, *The Eruption of Mount St Helens*, became a popular documentary.

Find out more

Further reading

Awesome Forces of Nature: Violent Volcanoes, Richard and Louise Spilsbury (Heinemann Library, 2004)

Expedition Earth: Volcano Evacuation, Dougal Dixon (Ticktock Media, 2004)

Horrible Geography: Violent Volcanoes, Anita Ganeri (Scholastic, 2004)

Natural Disasters: Volcanoes, Jacqueline Dineen (Hodder Wayland, 2002)

Turbulent Planet: Earth Erupts – Volcanoes, Mary Colson (Raintree, 2004)

Websites

www.geography-site.co.uk

A general geography site with lots of different sections on a range of topics.

www.geography.learnontheinternet.co.uk/topics/volcanoes

Factual information about volcanoes, with case studies to support the information covered.

volcano.und.edu

A website with information on lots of volcanoes around the world, news stories, 'volcano of the month', and lots of volcano images.

www.volcanolive.com

This website provides a comprehensive overview of the world's volcanoes. It has breaking news, live webcams, and a section on volcanology.

Map Active answers

Page 6: There are active volcanoes in east Africa which do not lie near a plate boundary. They lie near the centre of the African plate. There are also earthquake zones in southern and central Asia which are not close to a plate boundary.

Page 15: Planners and builders can look at the places where **lahars** flowed during the eruption and can try to avoid developing in these areas in future, as it is likely that any future lahars will follow a similar path. **Pyroclastic flows** are more difficult to plan around as they contain lots of gases and do not run over the landscape like lahars. However, the map shows that it would be wise to avoid development in any area close to the volcano.

Glossary

active volcano that is likely to erupt in the future

active zone area on Earth's crust where there is a lot of volcanic activity and/or earthquakes

adapt change to suit certain environmental conditions

barren where the conditions mean that nothing is able to grow

caldera large, basin-shaped crater formed when a volcano blows its top in a huge eruption

climate rainfall, temperature, and wind that normally affect a large area over a long period of time

constructive boundary where two of Earth's plates are pulling apart, and new crust is created in between

continent any one of the world's largest continuous land masses

crust hard outer layer of Earth

current liquid that flows constantly in one direction

destructive boundary where one of Earth's plates slides below the other and is destroyed as it enters the mantle

dormant volcano that has not erupted for a very long time, but which may erupt again

extinct volcano that has not erupted for millions of years and is unlikely to erupt again

fertile rich soil in which crops can grow easily

hot spot areas on Earth's crust which lie above very hot magma in the mantle

lahar river of mud formed when hot volcanic ash mixes with water, snow, or ice

lava hot molten rock that has erupted out of a volcano

magma hot molten rock that lies below the surface of Earth

magma chamber area in the mantle, underneath a volcano, where magma collects

mantle layer of hot, molten rock that lies below Earth's crust

mineral substance that is formed naturally in rocks and earth, such as coal, tin, or salt

molten melted

parasitic cone small volcanic cone formed on the side of a larger volcano, where a side vent pushes to the surface

pioneer species first or earliest species to grow in an area

plate tectonics the movement of large plates over Earth's surface

pyroclastic flow fast, explosive flow of volcanic ash, gases, and rocks

supervolcano huge volcano, mostly underground, whose eruption would affect the whole world

tectonic plate giant piece of Earth's crust that moves slowly over the mantle

trigger event that sets something or another chain of events in motion

vent opening of a volcano that lava, gas, and steam escape from

volcanologist scientist who studies volcanoes

Index